21 DAYS
of
Positive Living

Journal

A GUIDE TO POSITIVE WELL BEING

CRYSTAL M. MORRIS
— & —
ABENI C. SCOTT

Foreword by Chad Rowe

First Printing: 2018

Printed in the Unites States of America

Cover design by Canva

Interior design by Canva, Arty, Julie and Crystal M. Morris

Authors photo by Bethany Carpio

ISBN 978-1-790-72681-3

21 Days of Positive Living

Killeen, TX 76542

21daysofpositiveliving@gmail.com

Ordering Information:

Special discounts are available on quantity purchases by corporations, associations, educators, and others. For details, contact the publisher at the above listed address.

U.S. trade bookstores and wholesalers: Please contact 21 Days of Positive Living Tel: (254) 791-5815; or email 21daysofpositiveliving@gmail.com.

This Journal Belongs To:

_____

WHAT OTHERS ARE SAYING ABOUT *21 DAYS OF POSITIVE LIVING*

21 Days of Positive Living is a positive journaling tool to help with negative thinking or abate an attack or challenge negative thoughts. It counters the negative; however, there will always be an opposite. For example, if you are down, the only way you can go is up. Do the opposite of what is negative. If you don't like where you are going, stop and do the opposite of that—what you want. It's like a road map to where you want to go in life. It's like driving and navigating your life by using positive journaling. Think of negative thoughts as people. How can you escape the negative thoughts to break free?

Positive journaling is similar to narrative therapy, it allows you to write your script, your story. And rewriting your story gives you power. You have the power to change the situation instead of it changing you. You have the power to change the ending of your story. *21 days of Positive Living* will help you start living the life you always wanted!

Shai Evans, Ph.D.
Clinical Psychology

Thank you to our Father in Heaven who gave us the permission, wisdom and courage to write this journal. And to every person with whom I have crossed paths, this journal is for you.

FOREWORD

I have had the privilege of witnessing firsthand Crystal's growth both professionally and spiritually over the last several years, from the perspective of her Pastor.

Crystal consistently models one of my absolute favorite scriptures ~ Ephesians 3:16-21.

"I ask him to strengthen you by his Spirit—not a brute strength but a glorious inner strength—that Christ will live in you as you open the door and invite him in. And I ask him that with both feet planted firmly on love, you'll be able to take in with all followers of Jesus the extravagant dimensions of Christ's love. Reach out and experience the breadth! Test its length! Plumb the depths! Rise to the heights! Live full lives, full in the fullness of God. God can do anything: you know—far more than you could ever imagine or guess or request in your wildest dreams! He does it not by pushing us around but by working within us, his Spirit deeply and gently within us".

Moreover, it has always been Crystal's desire to empower others to live the abundant life that Christ died for us all to have. It has been said that it takes 21 days to form a habit and I firmly believe that this 21-day devotional journal will be the road map necessary in fostering a tremendous move of God in the lives of those that will daily apply the Word of God to their lives.

I read recently that *depression* is the number one mental illness in the United States, however, we have the antidote for depression, the precious Word of God: and as believers, it is our mandate from God to share His Word, His Will and His Way. We can no longer sit back passively or allow our friends, co-workers and neighbors to be guided by the pressures of various social media platforms, thus, dictating how they will think, act or feel in any given situation.

The late Pastor Adrian Rogers said, "If Satan can't make you bad, he'll make you busy". So often we get so distracted getting busy with work that we forget being busy is not the goal, productivity is the goal. How do we glorify God with our lives if all we do is going from sun up to sun down franticly marking off things off a "to do list" that is as long as our arm, only to fall into bed at night feeling unproductive, unfulfilled and under-valued? If our tasks are not managed properly, we can be robbed of a sense of extraordinary peace.

I sense that every person who connects with this 21-day devotional journal will have a divine appointment with the Lord, as He retrains each reader to think more like HIM.

Chad Rowe

Senior Pastor, Destiny World Outreach Center

INTRODUCTION

The vision of this 21-Day Journal was birthed from the destinies of two souls meeting, becoming friends and deciding to collaborate for the sake of humanity. Crystal and Celeste both delight in positive living and the thought thereof. We both share a deep passion for people and helping them out of circumstances that may or may not have been their doing.

21 Days of Positive Living is comprised of seven essential topics. We chose these because we firmly believe that, in order to think positive, you must be in a positive state of mind. Life brings about challenges that you never see coming. Experiences come as early as you can remember and before you know it, thought patterns have been stitched in your brain and your environment is now your social norm. 21 Days of Positive Living gets you back on track. It contains numerous quotes on Gratitude, Anger, Happiness, Relationships, Wisdom, Self-Worth, and Positive Wellbeing, which have been designed as food for your brain to help transform your mind into the healthy mind it was intended to be. In this journal, you have the power and flexibility to choose which lessons are best for you to explore first. Or, you may start from the beginning and read in a chronological order from start to finish. Nevertheless, each topic is comprised of a 21-day journey. Why 21 days? Because research says it takes 21 days to form a habit. We decided to break it down for you and provide you a point of reference to help you when life hands you lemons. At the end of the 21 days for each lesson, it is our hope you will have formed good habits that will afford you a more positive life.

What a better time as now to live your best life! Allow 21 Days of Positive Living to show you how.

SPECIAL INSTRUCTIONS

A healthy mindset generates a hefty balance in individuals that gives them power over their own situations. In this book, we have chosen positive quotes for you to journal and meditate on, so as to help you live a less stressed life. We implore you to take time to journal your thoughts in the present moment. Your thoughts may not be our thoughts, however, we challenge you to examine your thinking and write your positive thoughts for each quote on the lines provided. Your response is just that simple. Never reject or suppress your feelings. You are welcome to revisit any response for an assessment and revise your original response as you journal. Have fun making a happy journal.

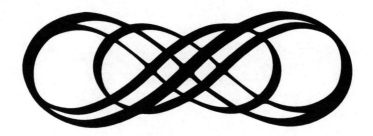

Contents

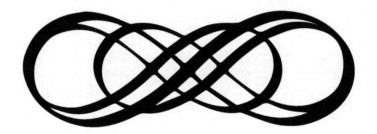

GRATITUDE

THE HEART OF GRATITUDE

Date _____   **Day 1**

Staying open to surprise packages often leads to surprise joys.
-Lynette Lewis

When we are open to life's surprises we can experience the joys of life with a little more gratitude. Life will bring a lot of surprises, so you must be open and prepared for what may come. By nature, I am a planner and an organizer, and as such, I like to know what is coming ahead so as to plan accordingly. On the other hand, I do like to be surprised in relationships with gifts, acts of service, surprise trips or quality time. But then there are bad surprises that come up and we get caught off guard and have to roll with the punches. When this happens, having a heart of gratitude will help you to focus so as to find the positive out of a negative situation. So always stay positive through putting your attention on positive experiences.

Date _____   **Day 2**

Feeling gratitude and not expressing it is like wrapping a present without giving it.
-William Arthur Ward

To tap into your abundance, you must have an attitude of gratitude. Wake up every morning and say out loud, "Thank you"! Set a daily alarm to remind yourself to thank God or the Universe for allowing you to petition them. I begin every prayer with "Thank you" and, in return, more is given to me. The more I give is the bigger my assignment gets. For unto whomsoever much is given, of him shall much be required (Luke 12:48; KJV). Don't hold on to wrapped presents, give them to whom they were first intended for. In the same way that wrapping precedes giving, thanking precedes receiving.

Date _____   Day 3

Gratitude makes sense of our past, brings peace for today, and creates a vision for tomorrow.
-Melody Beattie

Having a heart for gratitude makes it a lot easier to go through life. It helps you to appreciate the places in your life that were not so good, the low places of defeat and the struggles that seem like they would never end. When we can recognize the growth in our lives and where we come from, only then can we plan to live for tomorrow with hope. The kind of hope that shatters doubt and uncertainty. With a new level of certainty for your future you can begin to dream bigger and not live in fear. Today, every struggle means something to me because I had to labor and work for everything I have now. So when you arrive at a certain level of success, never forget where you came from, but remember the grind and the road to your success.

Date _____   ***Day 4***

I'm grateful for my former bullies, they taught me the immature
things not to do, and to stand up for myself.
-Keyondra White

Giants do fall. Why run before you even know if the pitbull has teeth? There are two types of people in the works. Those who fear and the fearless. You might be thinking bullies are the fearless ones—but that's wrong! Never allow someone else's fear become your fear. You be fearless, stand with your h3 (head held high) and h3 (hold his/her hand) again. Say to them, "I love you and thank you". This will leave them in utter shock and make them forget the reason they came after you in the first place. The opposite of fear is always love, the biggest packaged gift you can give an enemy is gratitude and love.

Date _____   *Day 5*

*Gratitude consists of being more aware of what you have than
what you don't.*
-Author Unknown

We often focus on the things we don't have because we are constantly
looking at other individuals and comparing ourselves to them. Keep
your eyes on your path and journey and set goals for yourself. Putting
things in perspective and viewing life well no matter how worse it gets
is an attitude of gratitude. I always remember that there is someone
out there that is less fortunate than I am and that I don't need to complain about the small things. Taking time to self-reflect on my life has
been eye-opening and beneficial to my overall happiness. Gratitude
has made me who I am today—empathic, compassionate, and caring.

Date _____   Day 6

When you arise in the morning, think of what a precious privilege
it is to be alive—to breathe, to think, to enjoy, to love.
-Marcus Aurelius

Live life to the fullest. We don't know when it will be our last time. Be happy in the moment. Be thankful for being alive. We have to start appreciating our loved ones while they are still with us. Cherish all the good times and happy memories and hold on to them. Because one day you may wake up and all you'd have will be just that—memories. The life we knew with that person is gone and all we have left is the memories. When you arise in the morning give thanks and pray and meditate. Mindfulness meditation can help you reduce worries and focus on the present life you are living.

Date _____   **Day 7**

Be thankful for what you have; you'll end up having more.
-Oprah Winfrey

Rising up to say "thank you" is how you ought to start your day. God or the Universe appreciates hearing from you at the break of day. Your thankfulness attracts thankful acts that are given out daily. You only have one job and that is to say "Thank You" first. The importance of having more is to give to others—this is also another blessing. When the Universe sees a giving heart of gratitude, it multiplies it's giving to you, leaving you wallowing in an abundant overflow. The power of the overflow is like a never-ending volcano erupting with hot lava. Now that's hot!

Date _____   ***Day 8***

As we express our gratitude, we must never forget that the highest appreciation is not to utter words, but to live by them.
-John F. Kennedy

Following through is important when you give a commitment to someone. Being a person of your word means everything. People remember what you say and don't do. When people don't feel the appreciation or it is not genuine, they will not connect with you. The character of a person is on the line at this point. I like to be a woman of my word because at the end of the day, if you want others to support you and work with you, being reliable and dependable are all valuable assets to possess. Make every word count that comes out of your mouth and live by them!

Date _____   *Day 9*

The hardest arithmetic to master is that which enables us to count
our blessings.
-Eric Hoffer

How do I love thee? Let me count the ways (Elizabeth Barrett Browning). Our blessings are always never ending and too much to count and that's what we must remember on days we feel like the world is against us and our prayers are being unanswered. There's always someone less fortunate; not that it will make you feel better, but the point is to remember the blessings you've already received and believe in those still to come. When you discover this, go back and help the less fortunate or intercede for them in prayer.

Date _____   *Day 10*

At times, our own light goes out and is rekindled by a spark from another person. Each of us has cause to think with deep gratitude of those who have lighted the flame within us.
-Albert Schweitzer

Discouragement and hopelessness will creep in like a thief in the night. Friends, family, or co-workers that encourage us to do our best can ignite that flame within us. It can turn the light back on that has been dimed. It is always nice to have someone else you least expect to say kind words of affirmation to brighten your day or encourage you to get moving on with your dreams and aspirations. Because when life hits us hard and we get knocked down, we sometimes need a helping hand to rise back up. Like Andria Day sings, "I'll rise up", her song inspires so many people to overcome obstacles and to keep trying despite the failure. It has inspired me as well as my faith in God.

Date _____   *Day 11*

Prayers of gratitude are powerful tools for wellness.
-Christiane Northrop

Your body and all it's 2000 body parts (Lever, 1985) function all day and every day for you. Thanking them daily can do the body good. Thank your eyes for vision and leading you where you need to go; your nose for being able to smell pleasant scents; your ears that bring through sweet sounding music; your head that sits high on your shoulder, and a neck that holds it up; a chest that beats a joyful heart; a full stomach, legs to take you where you want to go, feet to wash before his presence, a temple created by God. And lastly, the brain for controlling it all and doing what you tell it to do.

Date _____   **Day 12**

*The deepest craving of human **nature** is the need to be appreciated.*
-William James

Practicing gratitude is a great way to show someone your appreciation, while improving the quality of your relationship. (therapist-aid). Showing interest in one is a great way to show appreciation. Giving compliments is also a good way to improve showing appreciation as well. Just letting someone no they look nice today or thanking them for a job well done is showing appreciation. Doing some act of kindness for an individual is showing gratitude and that you care about that individual's feelings. Make a conscious effort to do something nice for no reason other than to help. You will be surprised how doing an act of kindness can turn around the day for you and your recipient.

Date _____   ***Day 13***

Nothing new can come into your life unless you are grateful for what you already have.
-Michael Bernard

The prerequisite for doing better is being a good steward over what's already been given to you. You will not receive that new car you want until you maintain the one you currently have. If you want a new house, clean up the one you now live in. If you want to be married, be kind to the potential prospects. You want a better job, show up on time to the one you have already and if you want a better life, be present in the one you are living in right Now.

Date _____   ***Day 14***

Be thankful for what you have; you'll end up having more. If you concentrate on what you don't have, you will never, ever have enough.
-Oprah Winfrey

Every day brings a combination of good and bad experiences. Unfortunately, the human brain tends to focus more heavily on the bad experiences while forgetting or discounting the good experiences. For example, we're more likely to remember one awkward social interaction over hundreds of normal interactions. (Therapist aid – positive journaling) When we focus on the negative things in life, we push the positive things to the side. Magnify the positive experiences or events in our life and the negative will become smaller. Making a point to recognize positive experiences no matter how small can help to improve our mood. Practice by recording three positive events at the end of each day.

Date _____   ***Day 15***

For every success in your life there must be a price to be paid; sacri-
fice writes the checks.
-Pastor Marla Rowe

Hard work will pay off. Everything you work for seems like it isn't worth it in the beginning, it seems like it's all in vain. You spend countless hours pouring into others, sowing seeds that appear not to be growing, which is supposed to harvest into what was promised to you. Well that's just it, remembering the goal is what motivates you to get up every day taking baby steps to help you get to your goal. All things come with a price, nothing in life is free except for the best things like "Gratitude". Saying thank you and being appreciative of things—that's free. All your challenging work and sacrifice will prove rewarding and literally pay you every day of your life.

Date _____   ***Day 16***

He is a wise man who does not grieve for the things which he has
not, but rejoices for those which he has.
-Epictetus

Focus on the positive experiences in your life and you will increase your overall happiness. The more positive things that we meditate on is the more optimistic we become about life. "The key to building happiness is for one to let go of what is negative in life; the other is to strengthen what is positive. Mainstream psychology focuses largely on the first strategy; Positive Psychology emphasizes the second" (Martin Seligman). Positive Psychology is the scientific study of positive human functioning that enables individuals and communities to thrive (International Positive Psychology Association). It focuses on positive emotions (joy, hope, and serenity), positive individual traits (compassion, optimism, and resilience), and positive institutions such as families, social, relationships, communities.

Date _____   ***Day 17***

If the only prayer you say in your life is thank you, that would suffice.
-A.H. Maslow

Thank you says more than any gift ever. We tend to think we have to shower people with money, material and tangible things in order to receive back. People know when gestures are not genuine. You don't have to live in a world where if someone buys you something, you have to buy them one in return. The reward is a genuine smile and a thank you. The biggest thank you are the ones given to your source. You will always get back what you put out. Saying "thank you" just once will give you many things to say thank you for.

Date _____   *Day 18*

Gratitude turns what we have into enough.
– Anonymous

When we are thankful and appreciative of all that we have, only then can we truly began to live. Giving thanks and finding positive experiences in our life helps us to enjoy life more. Though we may complain, just stop and take a moment to think about all of the things that you have, whether big or small. Keeping a journal of the things we are grateful for helps improve our mental well-being. Journaling about what we are grateful for can help reduce stress, increase happiness, and improve self-esteem. Writing at least two times a week about what you are grateful for will be beneficial to your overall well-being in a positive way.

Date _____   **Day 19**

Find the good and praise it.
-Alex Haley

In life there are many good things surrounding us. When you find yourself in a not so good mood, go outside, and you'll realize that it is in the simplest places you will find joy and peace. Trees, flowers, birds, grasses, leaves swaying from the wind, ponds, lakes, oceans, people, sand, a stop sign, a wooded bench, a fire hydrant, a dog chasing a squirrel, and children playing without a care in the world. O, that's good and worthy to be praised!

Date _____   ***Day 20***

Gratitude unlocks the fullness of life. It turns denial into acceptance, chaos to order, confusion to clarity. It can turn a meal into a feast, a house into a home, a stranger into a friend.
-Melody Beattie

When we are thankful we can experience life to the fullest. We may be in denial about something bad that has happened in our life and having a hard time accepting it. However, the good news is that having a heart of gratitude brings positive vibes and positive energy to us. It brings about a peace and a sense of calm and serenity. Gratitude makes you realize that when you are wrong you can humble yourself and possibly mend friendships or relationships. Gratitude can turn negative energy into positive energy. It can quiet the storms in your life and bring the joy that we seek every day.

Date _____   **Day 21**

*If you concentrate on finding whatever is good in every situation,
you will discover that life will suddenly be filled with gratitude, a
feeling that nurtures the soul.*
-Rabbi Harold Kushner

As a deployed soldier, it was hard leaving America to go to a land
where people didn't want you. Leaving back family that depended on
you and stressed out because you're constantly in harm's way. But soon,
I realized every girl from my neighborhood didn't get to experience
the life I was living. How many people can say they experienced life
this close to the promised land? It is in the wilderness that God speaks
and visions are birthed. I am thankful for every foreign land God sent
me. The same can apply for you. When it's foreign to you, embrace it
and listen closely to your instructions.

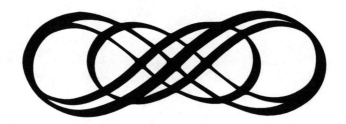

ANGER

NO MORE ANGER

Date _____   ## Day 1

Letting go of past hurts and failures in your life is accepting your present.
-Crystal Marie

When we stay in the present we don't dwell on the past hurts, disappointments or shortcomings. The past can't be changed, so when we live in the past it stunts our growth and hinder our ability to grow and be successful. Practicing mindfulness meditation helps you to stay in the present. Naturally our mind is going to drift and wander, however, with mindfulness meditation it allows us to be in a state of nonjudgmental awareness of what's happening in the present moment, including the awareness of one's own thoughts, feelings, and senses (Therapist Aid). Similar to the serenity prayer, we can ask God to grant us the serenity to accept the things we cannot change, the courage to change the things we can, and the wisdom to know the difference. I found this to be helpful in letting go of the past and to move forward to my future.

Date _____ Day 2

Sometimes I get to the point of frustration that I just become silent.
-Abantika Roy

There are times when silence will just not do. If you don't know how to stand up for yourself or express yourself in a manner that lets people know how they have made you feel, it will make matters worse for you. Suppressing your anger only turns into pain that you later don't understand, and the anger just continues to build. And when it escalates, that level of anger gets you into trouble. Because the fact of the matter is, it will later come out in a way you won't be able to control it. Managing your anger helps you to forgive immediately, see things differently, solve problems, as well as make healthy and wise decisions, which enable move closer to your destiny.

Date _____   *Day 3*

When you accept forgiveness and walk in freedom, then can you find hope for tomorrow.
-Crystal Marie

Forgiveness is a process where someone who has been wronged chooses to let go of their resentment, and treat the wrongdoer with compassion. Forgiveness does not mean forgetting or condoning the wrongdoing, granting legal mercy, or reconciling a relationship (Therapist Aid). I learned a long time ago that unforgiveness only hurts the person holding on to it. When we hold on to painful events or situations, we slow down the healing process. However, when we choose to forgive, forgiveness can reduce symptoms of depression, anxiety, and resentment.

Forgiveness has a lot of positive outcomes.

Date _____   *Day 4*

He who angers you, conquers you.
-Elizabeth Kenny

Anger is and is not a terrible thing. How we react to it is when it becomes bad. Mankind has made it what it is today by not managing the emotions that come with it. It is important that you diligently remove that thorn from your side in the most positive manner. Beat anger like it stole something from you, but smartly. Take back what it has stolen from you, but intelligently. Winning this battle will allow you to conquer battles to follow. The opposite of love is fear and living in fear turns into anger. Fear not and love plenty; for the real battle is not yours but the Lords.

Date _____   ***Day 5***

Never be in a hurry; do everything quietly and in a calm spirit. Do not lose your inward peace for anything whatsoever, even if your whole world seems upset.

-Francis de Sales

Often times, our world is turned upside down by chaos of the day or the unexpected happenings and our peace is interrupted. When this happens, what do you do? I find it helpful to re-center myself by doing mindfulness meditation exercises, such as the five senses, so as to ground myself in the present. From there I am able to let go of the negative and focus on the positive things in my life. Mindfulness meditation helps to slow down the racing thoughts in our mind. Calming your spirit takes practice and skills to redirect negative thoughts into alternate positive thoughts. The good news is, with practice and patience, having a calm, peaceful mind is obtainable.

Date _____   ***Day 6***

Where there is anger, there is always pain underneath.
-Eckhart Tolle

What have you not forgiven yourself for? What have you not forgiven someone else for? What are you not letting go that is keeping you from walking into your greatness? Who hurt you? Who are you hurting because of this? Hurt people, hurt people. Do you have an interest in hurt people? When you have healed from all your hurt, it is your assignment to go back and help someone else heal from their pain.

Date _____   **Day 7**

Acceptance is the road to peace—letting go of the worst, holding on to the best, and finding the hope inside that continues throughout life.
-Regina Hill

Sometimes, acceptance is hard for several reasons. When forgiveness is lacking, it's difficult at times to reason what happened or might have gone wrong or why expectations have not been met. Basically you have to let go of failures and hurts and find peace from within to really start living. Keep hope alive and let it flow like a river. Know that true acceptance is letting go of pain that is hindering you from thriving in life. It's like being stuck in a negative state of mind with negative emotions harboring on the inside. When we are in the stage of acceptance we are at the end of the grief cycle ready to live again.

Date _____   **Day 8**

Depression is anger that you turn on yourself.
-Dr. Craig K. Polite

If left untreated, any illness will wreak havoc on your body. In this case, ignored depression will turn into anger. Don't ever allow yourself to fall in a helpless circumstance because you think you don't have control over yourself or anything for that matter. People like having control over others; it's easy to control a victim than a healed revolving person (Union, G 2018). From your pain, no one has the right to have their hand on your life. Reclaim your power so you can get to the good stuff—your greatness.

Date _____   ***Day 9***

Forgiveness is looking at the pain, learning the lessons it has produced, and understanding what we have learned.
-Judith Mammay

Forgiveness is a process where someone who has been wronged chooses to let go of their resentment and treat the wrongdoer with compassion. Sometimes that is hard to do. It is choosing to let go of the hurt and finding the positive out of the situation in order to move forward in your life. It doesn't mean that you have to reconcile the relationship with the offender, but to learn lesson behind the hurt and learn more about you as an individual. Turn your tragedy into a triumph and you may be able to help someone else through their difficult times. You can forgive a person and yet in no way believe or accept that their actions were appropriate. Unforgiveness only keeps us stuck in negative painful emotions that prevent us from true healing and relieving symptoms of depression, anxiety, resentment or rumination of what happened. Let go and let the healing take place!

Date _____   *Day 10*

For every minute you remain angry, you give up sixty seconds of peace of mind.

-Ralph Waldo Emerson

When you realize you have built up anger, you have only one job and that is to get rid of it. Forgiveness is peace, forgiveness is happiness, forgiveness is joy, forgiveness is life, forgiveness is healing, forgiveness is liberty, forgiveness is the wounded being made whole, forgiveness is freedom, forgiveness is independence forgiveness is love!

Date _____   *Day 11*

When you're confronted with turmoil, respond with serenity. It will lift you to a higher level of experience and accomplishment… accomplishment comes more surely when your efforts are calm and your spirit is peaceful.
-Ralph S. Marston, Jr.

Many of you know the serenity prayer. To paraphrase the prayer, basically it is saying that you should focus on the things that you can control and not the things that you can't. Things out of our control can cause us to worry to no end and, as a result, cause restlessness and turmoil. Finding calmness and peace means to be aware of your emotions in the present moment, processing them and then letting go of the negative emotions leading to the road of peace. Mindfulness meditation helps one to find that peace in the present moment. It doesn't judge our thoughts, but just acknowledges they are there and then releases them out of our mind; especially the negative thoughts.

Date _____   ***Day 12***

Forgiveness does not change the past, but it does enlarge the future.
-Paul Boose

Forgiveness is self-care for your soul. We spend time cleaning up our homes, decluttering and organizing during spring cleaning and some of us even try and clean up other's issues instead of focusing more on ourselves. Unforgiveness is a huge mess that takes a long time to clean, if it goes unnoticed, and worst still, if it goes ignored. The best way to get rid of the mess is to clean it up as soon as you notice it. Forgive the person that has hurt you, they are hurt themselves; forgive the person you can't even remember the reason for which you are mad at them; forgive the person that keeps you up at night. forgiving allows you to do the work you were called to do which leads to a promising and meaningful future.

Date _____   **Day 13**

Every day we have plenty of opportunities to get angry, stressed or offended. But what you're doing when you indulge these negative emotions is giving something outside yourself power over your happiness. You can choose to not let little things upset you.
-Joel Osteen

When we choose to give our energy into negative vibes or allow someone to make us mad, as it were, we are choosing to give that person power over how we feel and let them dictate our lives. We have the power to control our emotions and, thus, choose to be angry or happy. Everything is a choice. ***"Great peace have they which love thy law and nothing shall offend them"*** (Psalms 119:165; KJV). What we choose to meditate on can affect us in a positive or negative way, so always choose to meditate on the positive things and find solutions to the conflict. Put out good, positive vibes!

Date _____   **_Day 14_**

Our emotions are the driving powers of our lives.
-Earl Riney

If you can't manage your emotions, managing your life will be just as difficult. When I'm mad at myself all the time, it makes it so easy to be mad at others or the spouse and kids. Think about it, why do we yell at our children who look just like their father or mother who walked out on us? Or things just didn't work out and now you hate him or her and are now stuck raising the child alone who is the smitten image of them. Are we mad at the child too now? The power of managing emotions is what drives a happy life.

Date _____   *Day 15*

Anger and intolerance are the enemies of correct understanding.
-Mahatma Gandhi

Anger can be caused by a misunderstanding. Learning to gain understanding before seeking to be understood can resolve disputes and anger. Often times when we are angry we don't stop to ask ourselves why we are angry and if we may have misunderstood something. The hard part is listening when you are angry. When you are upset the last thing you want to do is try to understand and see the perspective of the other person. Managing your anger is key that can lead to great listening and understanding of the other person. Take a time out and cool down and think about your emotions, why you are so upset and if there is a good reason to be upset.

Date _____   *Day 16*

If you spend your time hoping someone will suffer the consequences for what they did to your heart, then you're allowing them to hurt you a second time in your mind.
-Shannon L. Alder

Your thoughts create things that will move you into action, whether it is good or horrific acts. I've learned to give people what they don't have. So instead of talking bad about them or wishing ill-will on someone who has wronged you, pray for them and give them more kindness and all the love you can afford. When you do this, two things happen: they eventually are delivered from the grief and malice and treat you the way you demand for them to treat you; and second, you are rewarded for your kind act and the Universe gives you what you give out and God rewards you in ways that leave you in awe.

Date _____   **Day 17**

Anger is the enemy of non-violence and pride is a monster that
swallows it up.
-Mahatma Gandhi

Anger often times brings about violent behavior, therefore, it is the opposite of being nonviolent. It's hard to admit when we are being prideful because, with a negative connotation, pride refers to a foolishly and irrationally corrupt sense of one's personal value, status or accomplishments. The King James Bible verse of Ephesians 4:26 says that we can be angry but sin not. When pride gets in the way of expressing our anger in a healthy way, we remain in a selfish place, making it difficult to let go of the negative emotion. Anger is a secondary emotion. So finding out the primary emotion is key to living and walking in positivity.

Date _____   *Day 18*

A heart filled with anger has no room for love.
-Joan Lunden

Love feels good. Love is happy. In the toughest situations, love fills the room. Love universally is represented by a heart shape. People want and need love to survive. Love is the answer in most situations. If we remember this and make love the answer, when anger is drowning us, we will find that love is the only lifeguard and life vest we need to save us from drowning in the depth of anger.

Date _____   **Day 19**

Bitterness is like cancer. It eats upon the host. But anger is like fire.
It burns it all clean.
-Maya Angelou

Bitterness and anger usually come together as a pair. Bitterness is anger and disappointment at being treated unfairly. Resentment is like walking around being upset at the world because of a past event that has left you hurt, scarred, and jaded. Consuming fire can purify things at very high temperatures. When anger is expressed in a healthy way, it could be like fire, to burn up or prevent bitterness. Bitterness eats away at your heart and causes hate and numbness to emotions. Bitterness is like being mad at the world and seeking vengeance on anyone that comes in its path. Break down the wall of anger and bitterness before it begins by expressing your negative emotions assertively.

Date _____   Day 20

Never respond to an angry person with a fiery comeback, even if he deserves it. Don't allow his anger to become your anger.
-Bohdi Sanders

Never allow someone else's fear to become yours. Anger stems from fear. Racism, womanism, hate, bullying, rejection, abandonment all start with fear. When this type of fear fires at you, don't react to it by returning the favor and giving someone what you think they deserve, but rather respond to it by giving it what it needs, which is love and kindness. The reward is much bigger, better and brighter (Pastor Chad Rowe).

Date _____   ***Day 21***

Holding on to anger is like grasping a hot coal with the intent of
throwing it at someone else; you are the one who gets burned.
-Buddha

When we hold on to negative emotions like anger, others such as anxiety, depression, resentment can always settle in and cause us to be stuck. Being stuck in negative emotions like anger can lead to bitterness and unforgiveness, and as a result, you only hurt yourself. Unforgiveness only hurts the person holding onto to the hurtful emotions of the past. Letting go of negative emotions is healthy and necessary to live a positive, productive, thriving life. The person we are harboring negative emotions for is rarely affected. Releasing the hurt, the anger is healthy and beneficial for your physical health as well. Holding on to anger can cause stress to your physical body as well as spiritually. Remember what we put out into the atmosphere is what we will have returned to us. So put out good positive vibes!

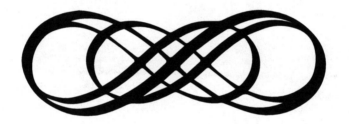

HAPPINESS

HAPPINESS COMES FROM WITHIN

Date _____   **Day 1**

Joy is not in things; it is in us.
-Richard Wagner

When we finally realize that true happiness comes from within and that we have a choice to be happy, then we can shift our mindset and have an exuberance about life. Material things do come and go; so that means our joy is not genuine or stable if it's based on those. No one can physically take away your joy if it's rooted on the inside of you. Joy means to have great pleasure and happiness. Building happiness on the inside requires practice and maintenance. We can build happiness on the inside by meditating on positive things in our lives, positive quotes and much more. *"A merry heart does good, like medicine, but a broken spirit dries the bones"* (Proverbs 17:22; NKJV).

Date _____   ***Day 2***

You will be as exactly happy as you decide.
-Author Unknown

You have the right to choose happy. Allowing a negative situation to determine if you smile or laugh for the day is all in your hands. Happiness is a lifestyle and a state of mind. I'm saying you must keep a permanent smile on your face even if something has happened because, although a temporary emotion is affecting you in the moment, you have the choice to move on. Don't stay in a sad place and choose happy. Helping others is my happy place.

Date _____   *Day 3*

True happiness must come from within you. You will find happiness by letting your conscience guide you—listen to it; follow it. Your conscience is the key to your happiness.
-Poynter Taylor

The inward voice on the inside of us is who we really are. Feed your inward voice with positivity and as a result, you will find yourself on the road to true happiness. Ultimately, if we are not happy with who we are on the inside, no one else will be either. Happiness is contagious, it gets deep down inside the soul of a person and when transferred, it is a powerful, wonderful and an amazing feeling.

Date _____   *Day 4*

Stop looking for happiness in the same place you lost it.
-Author Unknown

If the things that once gave you joy doesn't anymore, get rid of it. If it's still lingering and tearing you up in pieces day by day, get rid of it. If it has left on its own, stop chasing it; wondering and worrying when it will return. Perhaps that's not where you lost it and it's someplace else. Do some soul searching and the answers are already within you. Happiness starts and ends with you, don't make the mistake of making your happiness the responsibility of someone else.

Date _____   **Day 5**

Happiness cannot come from without. It must come from within.
It is not what we see and touch or that which others do for us which
makes us happy; it is that which we think and feel and do, first for
the fellow and then for ourselves.
-Helen Keller

Positive thinking builds happiness. When we learn to meditate on positive things, such as positive quotes or positive experiences, our thoughts begin to shift, negative thoughts decrease and positive thoughts begin to be the norm and, as a result, we become happier. So happiness starts on the inside of us. We remove or take away material things; however, if you have that "unspeakable joy on the inside" that can't be taken away, we have to choose to give that joy away on the inside. That feeling of elation, the contentment would have to be given away freely. Doing for others also builds happiness and a heart of gratitude.

Date _____   *Day 6*

The happiness you feel is in direct proportion to the love you give.
-Oprah Winfrey

The more you love is the more love comes back to you. In the event when I am not feeling loved or it seems I am not loving, I have learned to open my heart and give what I think I'm not receiving and the Universe always gives back to me what I am giving. The more love you give is the more love comes back to you. This secret not only works with love, but happiness, joy, peace, wisdom, and negative emotions that try and take your power. Give more of what you want.

Date _____   Day 7

Happiness is a butterfly, which when pursued, is always just beyond your grasp, but which, if you sit down quietly, may light upon you.
-Nathaniel Hawthorne

Happiness is so close, it's within reach if we can just sit still enough to notice and recognize it. Sometimes we don't know how close we are until we need it the most. I remember a time when I was struggling to find that happiness and I knew it was close to me but I just couldn't grab it quick enough. Just like when you try to catch a butterfly; at that crucial moment right when you think you've caught it, it escapes. Now you are waiting on that next moment, opportunity, yet hopeful time to catch that happiness. When you catch it, hold on to it as long as you can. You never know when you will need that touch of joy to carry you through challenges. Hold happiness tight, close to your heart.

Date _____   ***Day 8***

*Happy is the man that finds wisdom and the man that gets under-
standing.*
-Proverbs 3:13

Wise and understanding people are happy? Yes. Why? Because it takes wisdom and understanding to realize where true happiness comes from. The wise can encounter circumstances, overcome and conquer obstacles in their own mess and go back and help someone else in their mess. The wise turns a mess into a message and writes a book about it in several translations so that it helps others in the entire world. Wise people look for ways to help others and impact the world. Wise people are servant leaders, problem-solvers, innovative and gamechangers. They make the world go round and, more importantly, respond to the things that bring only joy.

Date _____   **Day 9**

*There is only one way to happiness and that is to cease worrying
about things which are beyond the power of our will.*
-Epictetus

Mastering the art of letting go is genius. Letting go of things one has
no control of is an ongoing challenge for many people. It took me a
while to realize I was holding on to negative emotions, which had been
affecting my happiness. Bitterness, resentment, and vengeance are all
negative emotions that can dry up the happiness in your heart and
soul. Focus on the things you can control, like your behavior and emotions, and stay in the present moment. To be in the present moment
means to be mindful of your surroundings. It is learning to accept your
emotions and move forward in your mind. Mindfulness meditation
is paying attention on purpose to your thoughts and emotions non-
judgmentally and accepting things you cannot change; it also involves
processing how you feel and releasing the negative emotions. Letting
go takes intentional work and, when done correctly, can bring a tremendous amount of ease and peace.

Date _____   ***Day 10***

Folks are usually about as happy as they make their minds up to be.
-Abraham Lincoln

If your emotions are conformed to a certain way of feeling, it will not take long for your brain to copycat and soon your emotions and brain will make the same drumbeat. Thinking about happiness leads you to decide to be happy; deciding to be happy leads you to feel happy; feeling happy leads you to do "only" happy things. Think, decide, feel, do, and BE HAPPY!

Date _____   **Day 11**

*Be happy in the moment, that's enough. Each moment is all we
need, not more*
-Mother Teresa

Cherish the moments of happiness you receive. Be grateful for the small things and be content within. When we focus on our positive experiences and meditate on those times, we can have a continual pleasure of happy moments. Learn to be satisfied by thinking yourself happy. Think of all the things that you do have that's good and run with that thought. Focus on those merry thoughts and you will have happier moments.

To be happy, we must not be too concerned with others.
-Albert Camus

"Stay in your lane" is one of the best advice you could ever give any-one. While traveling, if the motorist starts paying attention to some-thing else, they'd obviously get distracted and if they're not careful a crash can take place. The crash could cause minor or major damages or, worse still, a fatal accident. To keep your happiness, don't worry about others. They must find their own happiness, you didn't give it to them and, more than likely, you didn't take it away from them to begin with. Don't cause a wreck because you're trying to fix something already broken and you don't have the right tools.

Date _____   ***Day 13***

Do more of what makes you happy.
Anonymous

Being happy is a choice. So choose wisely. That is, choose things that will make you happy. We all know what makes us happy and what keeps us in that happier place. Learning to build and maintain happiness takes intentional effort. Others have mastered this skill and they are always doing things that make them happy. It is learning to put yourself first sometimes. That can be a difficult task for many people. It's okay to say "no" to other people or things. How many of us suffer from trying to please people? No matter how much effort you take to please everyone, someone out there will still not be satisfied. At the end of the day, you are the only one that can turn on that happy spirit on the inside of you. We are in control of our emotions and how we feel.

Date _____   *Day 14*

Happiness is when what you think, what you say, and what you do are in harmony.
-Mahatma Gandhi

Happy thoughts encourage happy feelings; happy feelings encourage happy behavior. Let your thoughts, feelings and behavior sing in a beautiful harmony every day of your life. The power you hold is dependent upon the three being practiced (which means you are responsible for your happiness). When your happiness is held in your own hands, you don't ever look for it in anything or anyone else.

Wake up and be happy.
-Anonymous

Have you ever heard someone say, "I woke up on the wrong side of the bed?" I sometimes want to say, "well roll back over to the right side of the bed so you can be happy." Comically as it may seem, happiness comes from the inside and you can either turn it on or off. Learn to turn on that happy spirit, the bubbling joy on the inside. How you start your day is how you will finish your day. Wake with a positive mindset and if you don't, stop and take a moment in the hustle of your day, and let go of the negative feelings.

Date _____   ***Day 16***

The best way to pay for a lovely moment is to enjoy it.
-Richard Bach

The best things in life are free! As an adolescent, when hearing this for the first time, I had no idea what it meant. Ask me now and I'd probably say "Love." Love is free and so are lovely things, such as being present. Lovely moments can be found in the simplest things, like stopping to play with your daughter for five minutes on your way out the door for work and seeing the smile on her face; fixing the collar of your spouse's shirt because they asked, and sure, they could've very well done it themselves; or lying on a blanket outside and looking up at the sky and watching the clouds make shapes. And the only price to pay is to ENJOY IT.

Date _____   **Day 17**

A secret to happiness is letting every situation be what it is instead of what you think it should be.
Anonymous

Expectations are often left unmet when they are unrealistic. When we expect to receive happiness from our significant other, our family, our children and we don't get it, we are often left disappointed. Remember true happiness starts within us. Learning to focus on things in our control and cultivating happiness on the inside of us will help us to live a fulfilled life of hope and promise. *"Hope deferred makes the heart sick, but when the desire comes, it is a tree of life"* (Proverbs 13:12; NKJV).

Date _____   **Day 18**

Happy does not have to be only an Hour.
Abeni Celeste

Happy is the day when you wake up and declare it will be happy 24 hours, you will not allow anyone or anything to distract you from your goal for the day. You protect your environment from negative influences, demolish strongholds and arguments. You provide your spirit with positive impact, speak life over every situation and circumstance. Remember that mercy is renewed every morning and, because of this, you can wake up every day with new conquering powers to get right what you fell short of the day prior. Be content with Happiness. You deserve it.

Date _____   **Day 19**

If there's even a slight chance at getting something that will make you happy, risk it. Life's too short, and happiness is too rare.

-A. R. Lucas

At the end of the day when you find happiness, it is rare. So you have to hold on to it because you never know when you will see it again; if you will see it in this life time. I have learned that life is short and we have to cease the moment because tomorrow is not promised, so take advantage of life's happiness when it comes and enjoy every bit of it. We can create other happy moments in our lives but we have to be intentional. That is, building happiness on purpose. Doing things that will make you happy and maintaining happiness in your life.

Date _____   **Day 20**

No matter how good or bad life gets, wake up each morning grateful
you have one.
-Author Unknown

Happy is as happy does. Hang with happy people, sing and listen to happy music, decorate your space with happy things, wear happy colors (yellow, orange, green), think happy thoughts, have happy feelings, behave happily. Set your mind and determine that life is rather good, whether not-so-good or ugly happens. And don't forget to dance. Dancing is liberating, freeing and it makes you happy.

Date _____   **Day 21**

Happiness is loving every minute of who you are and where you are.
-Ilva Tua-Smith

In the words of Monica, one of the best R&B singers of my younger times, "I got Love all over me, I got Love all over me, because you (Love) have touched every part of me." You know sometimes you have to seek and sing a song in your spirit to help you get through tough days. Ilva and I recently recorded a broadcast where we reminded our tribe of women to be independent. Most women are very independent. Yes, you pay your own bills, live in your own home and make your own decisions, yet, lack independence in your mind, your happiness, your joy and love. Don't depend on others for your own happiness. Love yourself and you don't ever have to seek it from others. Love yourself and others will automatically love you back.

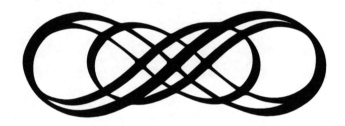

SELF-WORTH

LOVING WHO YOU ARE

Date _____   ***Day 1***

I am not my negative thoughts, I don't have to believe them… De-clutter the negative thoughts and invite the positive thoughts to stay.
-Crystal Marie

As humans, our minds are going to naturally wonder and some of our thoughts may be negative. The good news is we don't have to allow them to stay and get stuck in our minds. We have the power to choose what we mediate on or ruminate on. The key is to focus on positive thoughts by thinking positive. I found out that meditating on positive quotes daily and writing about what they mean to you is beneficial to the overall mood of individuals. Positive thinking practiced regularly can reduce symptoms of depression, anxiety, stress and even one's overall health will improve. So find those positive quotes to journal about and include positive affirmations as well.

Date _____   ***Day 2***

I will not hide who or what I am.
-Iyanla Vanzant

Until you deal with some things, such as lack of self-worth and low self-esteem, walking in your purpose will be difficult. Choose right this very moment to release yourself from the fears that have been holding you back. Perhaps you've never been informed or you have but just didn't listen. Hiding who you are is living afraid. Afraid that you've been told you can't and never will amount to anything because of something you did, or someone has done to you, afraid because of rejection, abandonment, or because of the need to be perfect. Perfectionism keeps you from your destiny; because you want everything to be perfect you either don't step out in faith or when you try it and fail you get so disappointed and never try again.

Date _____   *Day 3*

Depression is the result of a cognitive triad of negative beliefs regarding oneself, one's experience.
-Aaron T. Beck

What we meditate or think about is going to be manifested in our actions. What we think tells others who we are and what we are about. If you don't believe in yourself, who else will? Know who you are and what you stand for (e.g. values). I encounter a lot of people in my line of work that say they don't know who they are and what they want out of life. I often tell them to find their passion and likes and dislikes and use that as a baseline or guide. Trying out new things that you might be interested in. Also, doing things you are good at is a good indication you are on the right path. I was blessed earlier on in life to figure out what my passion was and what I was good at; like helping others or teaching for example. With prayer and meditation, I was able to find my career and so can you!

Date _____   **Day 4**

You are as much as you are right now.
–Yoruba Proverb

You are what you think. You are what you believe about yourself. You believe what you think about yourself. If you think and believe you are beautiful right now, you'll believe you can be beautiful later. If you believe you can achieve goals now, you'll believe it later. If you believe you can influence others now, you'll believe it later. If you believe you can impact the world, you'll believe it later. What you believe right now about yourself will determine your future actions. Future means the next minute, day, month, year, decade and years to come.

Date _____   **Day 5**

Fall in love with taking care of yourself. Mind, Body, Spirit.
                    –Author unknown

Self-care is an essential part of being successful. Learning to take time for yourself shows that you love and care about your own well-being and overall health. Self-care can be done anywhere with little expense. Self-care means finding life balance and taking care of yourself in the areas of your psychological, emotional, spiritual, personal, professional, and physical aspects. When we take care of our self, we can then be better to others we want to help such as loved ones, friends and family members. Being the best you can be is taking care of you first. That may sound selfish but, if you are no good, others around you can't really reap the fruit of your help. Be you and be your biggest supporter!

Date _____   **Day 6**

You may not know how to raise your self-esteem, but you know how to stop lowering it.
-Awo Osun Kunle

Live proud of who you are and what you bring to the table. You were made with unique gifts and were created to use them because no one can do it like you. It's so much easier to walk in the path chosen for you than to walk in someone else's. The moment you decide to stop lowering your self-esteem you will begin to raise it. Embrace yourself and then Celebrate being you. When you love yourself first, you make it easier for others to love you.

Date _____   ***Day 7***

*When we place our expectations in people, we are often let down
and left disappointed.*
-Crystal Marie

We are in control of our own destiny and how we live our life, who we spend our time with, and that means when we take responsibility for our own emotions we won't put unrealistic expectations on people. Being accountable for your emotions means you have control over them and can choose to feel disappointed, let down or happy. True happiness starts from within and is internal not external. Yes, we are human and we are going to experience negative emotions, such as disappointment, but we don't have to get stuck in the negative emotions that prevent us from moving forward. The key to letting go of negative emotions is staying in the present and recognizing them for what they are—negative—and release them and replace them with positive emotions. With practice, you can build your happiness and maintain it!

Date _____   **Day 8**

Love is never outside Ourselves; Love is within us.
-Louise Hay

Love who you are. Love is not where you lost it because real love cannot be lost. If love has left you, it was never yours to begin with, you were just borrowing it and didn't know it. True love is in you. So when love walks away, divorces you, breakup with you or mistreats you, you'll overcome because love for yourself is never lost. Love is on the inside of you. I love who I am, so therefore, I love all of me.

Date _____   *Day 9*

> *Be brave. Be strong. Don't give up. Expect God to get here soon.*
> -MSG Bible-Psalms 31:24

There was a time in my life when I was struggling in my faith and could not find balance and strength to persevere. I learned that building resiliency during tough times is a valuable asset for getting through and out of bad situations. My faith as well as focusing on the positive things that was going on in my life helped me to be brave, strong and not to give up when I wanted to throw in the towel. The death of my father was one of the hardest things to accept and push through. It was a dark place in my life where I felt lost and alone and I had to get back to the root of my faith and remember what God has done for me. But thank God, He showed up and never left me alone but was right there walking with me during the hopeless times of my life.

Date _____   **Day 10**

The best confidence booster is setting small realistic and achievable goals for yourself. It makes us feel good when we set out to do something and do get it done. I like to use the example of making your bed. If you are a person who never makes the bed, set a goal to complete this task first thing in the morning when you rise. Celebrate it, don't take it lightly and see what else you can get done. It's like the old saying, "when the going gets tough, the tough gets going." So, get it while the getting is easy!

Date _____   *Day 11*

*Acceptance is the heart's best defense, love's greatest asset, and the
easiest way to keep believing in yourself and others.*
-Regina Hill

Acceptance is the road to the reality of a situation, i.e., recognizing a
process or condition without attempting to change it or protest against
it. Understanding the situation logically and coming to terms emotionally with the situation is acceptance. Most people had to experience acceptance when they were dealing with some type of loss. For instance,
it could be the loss of a job (career), relationship, or even the death of
a loved one. According to Kübler-Ross, acceptance is the last stage in
the grief cycle. When we arrive at acceptance, we are now able to move
forward in our life. It's a time where you can be open to love again and
when your heart can start the healing process.

Date _____   *Day 12*

Somebody somewhere tricked you into believing there were certain things you could not do because of who you were.
-Iyanla Vanzant

"Lies! You are a lie and the truth is no part of you!" That's precisely what you are to say to the liars who want you to believe negative things about yourself. It's the enemy's tactic and the oldest trick in his book. Since when do we allow evil to become stronger than us (Tauriel)? The one who is in you is greater than the one who is in the world (1 John 4:4). I recently learned that bumblebees have no business flying with their huge bodies and thin wings, but they don't know that, hence, you see them flying everywhere unafraid and making others afraid. My mom taught me when I was a child "believe none of what you hear and only half of what you see."

Date _____   ***Day 13***

I am not discouraged, because every wrong attempt discarded is another step forward.
-Thomas A. Edison

Sometimes we have to take a step back to move forward with a goal or dream we are attempting to obtain. Don't be discouraged every time you fail. Look at failure as another step towards success. Learn from the things that did not work and perfect it for the next time. It's called resiliency. Pushing through tough times without giving up so easily is becoming resilient. I learned to become optimistic hopeful about my future and to think positive too. It has helped me to achieve many goals and make them become a reality. When we keep picking ourselves back up after failure, we are bound to find one success!

Date _____   Day 14

Don't be an Olympic Swimmer in Shallow waters. It's time to move.

-Ivy McGregor

It's time to move, move out, get going on something, got to move, break free, can't sit around for nothing and I got to change my ways, got to find some direction, stand out from the shadow and feel the light on my face (Janet Williams). You have in you what you need to succeed; your friends and family see it and they've told you, but you don't believe them. Come out of the shadows of others and step into your own light shining in you, you can swim in deeper waters than you think, the most precious jewels are far off into the deep.

Date _____   ***Day 15***

Believe in yourself and your dreams. You will soon realize that the future holds many promises for you. Remember… difficult times don't last forever.
-Geri Danks

I always say that the experiences we have are not all permanent. Let's view our bad or negative experiences as temporary one's that can change for the better. With positive thinking you can learn to view negative situations as learning points and keep it moving. Keep your eye on the prize of winning. It's like a race, who will continue and reach the finish line? Keep pressing until you achieve what you want out of life. We have the power to set the stage for our life's success. So what do you plan to do? Know who you are and you will know where you are going.

Date _____   **Day 16**

> ### *Jump, and Grow Wings on the way down. Johnny Wimbrey via Les Brown*

In this world you will take risk. Risk are fun and exciting if you keep telling yourself that. Birds are made to fly. Baby eagles get kicked out of their nests by the mama eagle to give them a little motivation to try. What will you do when this happens? Hit the ground and platter, hit the ground running, or grow your wings on the way down? The same applies to us. Leap! Jump out in faith, watch and witness the growing of your wings on the way down. I guarantee you will fly high. Lastly, go back and help someone else do the same.

Date _____   ***Day 17***

Self-esteem is as important to our well-being as legs are to a table. It is essential for physical and mental health and for happiness
-Louise Hart

Self-care plays a major part in building your self-esteem or self-worth. When take "me" time, we are showing ourselves love. When we show ourselves love and care it means we have some type of value for who we are and what we think about ourselves. So think highly of the person you are. You are your biggest supporter. Take time to show love to you on a regular basis. I have self-care Sunday's now. There was a time when I couldn't say no to people and I always wanted to help. I quickly became burnt out and was no good to them or myself. Finding balance in your life is important to maintaining your well-being, and that includes boosting your self-esteem and self-worth.

Date _____   *Day 18*

Future me eats little me as a vitamin every morning.
-Marshawn Evans Daniels

Little me will grow up one day and live the life that little me chose. Little me doesn't want to believe that future me can be great. So therefore, you must allow future me to eat away at little me. Vitamins give nourishment, replace and give you what you need to grow. Allow yourself to make mistakes and fail. If you fall five thousand times, get back up five thousand times. Falling brings maturity and success to your life. Focus on the big picture and your "why" so as to stay inspired.

No one can make you feel inferior without your consent.
-Eleanor Roosevelt

We teach others how we want to be treated. We are in control of our thoughts, emotions, and behaviors. Once you realize that, you will start choosing to let go of those negative emotions. Don't give away power or energy to people that choose to treat you as less. Know your worth. That means to figure out what your likes and dislikes are and to teach others that are in your inner circle as well as outer to know and value same things about you. We have a choice as per who we spend our time with and how, so spend time with positive, loving, supportive people that will encourage and uplift you in every way: emotionally, socially, physically, and spiritually.

Date _____   **Day 20**

Keep failing until you win, Learn from your losses.
-Slim Thug

The greatest part about failing is you learn what not to do the next time you try. I'm a firm believer that all situations have some good coming from it. All things work for the good of those who love God, who are the called according to his purpose. (Romans 8:28). I recall the first time I had this realization. I had a horrible boss and could not understand how and why they could have such a terrible disposition. I felt like I failed everyday going to work. I learned from that situation how not to be that type of "boss". That situation made me a passionate and servant leader who has been recognized by great leaders I look up too. Let your mindset be "even when I fail I win; therefore I always win". In the words of T Pain, "all I do is Win, Win, Win no matter what!"

All our Dreams can come true if we have the courage to pursue them.
-Walt Disney

Do your part and others will do theirs. In life, we don't pursue our dreams because we are afraid of them. We're afraid they are so big and that we don't trust ourselves to get them done. Believe you have what it takes to be successful and don't be afraid to do it alone. Not everyone is meant to go on the journey with you. In the words of Colin Powell, "it is lonely at the top". Be not afraid of those who will say to you, "No", close the door in your face, deceive you or not support you like you think they should, and more importantly, don't be afraid to fail. Failure means you just wrote the book on what not to do. We learn from mistakes; they are intended to help elevate us.

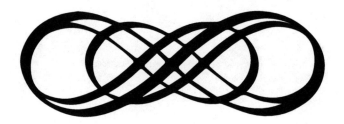

WISDOM

KNOWLEDGE IS POWER

Date _____   ***Day 1***

Living in the past mistakes will only hinder your faith walk in God and your potential to thrive in life.
-Crystal Marie

When we get stuck in past thoughts, events, experiences, it is difficult to move forward and experience the life God wants us to have; the abundant agape life. Ruminating on failures and shortcomings only brings about negative emotions and moods such as anxiety, depression and anger. Learning to let go of the past mistakes and failures allows us the opportunity to develop healthier positive emotions like joy, peace, and happiness. Once we let go of what should have happened or what we expected and accept the present, then can we truly live and gain everything God intends for us to have, that is, increase more and more. Learn the lesson from past mistakes and keep it moving!

Date _____   ***Day 2***

Living in the present is embracing your future.
-Crystal Marie

A year ago, I would not have understood this quote. In the book "Love is letting go of fear", it is explained so clearly. We believe all negative things that happened in our past will be the same for our future. This type of thinking will cause patterns and continue to repeat itself in your present. Worrying about the past and believing your future will turn out the same affects your present and, therefore, your mindset is your future is ruined without the possibility of change. However, when you live in the present by being conscious and enjoying the moment, seeing the beauty of what's in front of you, changing things you have control over and accepting what you cannot, it is then you begin to love, live and laugh out loud.

Date _____   *Day 3*

Accept and appreciate that you're the one most responsible for making your dreams come true. Choose your thoughts, because if you don't, you're still making a choice. Make the connection between your thoughts, your actions, and the results you're getting. Live your life consciously; don't just let your life live you.
-Donna Fargo

We are where we are today because of the choices we have made and things we have said and done. If you want something different in your life you have to be willing to do something different to chance the end results. Someone once told me that what you think is what you are going to say, and what you say tells me who you are as a person. So speak life, speak positive, because *"Death and life are in the power of the tongue"* (Proverbs 18:21; KJV). We are creative beings and have the power to create our own destiny. Know what you want out of life and take action to get the happy life you desire!

Date _____   ***Day 4***

Life opens opportunities to you, and you either take them or you stay
afraid of taking them.
-Jim Carrey

We tend to delay our good by thinking we can't receive all the promises on this Earth and that they are nonexistent; that is, we won't have those things until we are in Heaven. Words like: "it isn't meant to be;" "God will provide" (and, yes, things are meant to be; yes, He will provide, but we must act and activate faith); "I'll be alright, it's not my timing;" "I don't have time;" "if it's for me I'll wait for it to happen…" They are all excuses preventing us from acting out our dreams. I used to say that good things come to those who wait, and in some way, that is true, but you must work each day and wait. The Bible says faith without works is dead. Nothing will happen if you don't work. And a man that does not work does not eat. Let's makes sure we can eat for generations to come.

Date _____   *Day 5*

When one dream is on hold, go live others.
Lynette Lewis

Dreams may be delayed but not denied. Pursue your other goals that are obtainable at that time. Be productive in life and be a doer. That means to take action. Set goals and steps to obtain those goals. Creating a vision board with magazine pictures or just writing it out can help you reach goals faster and stay accountable as well as on track. Being accountable means to be responsible for your own behaviors or maybe just checking in with someone so that they can encourage you to follow through. If you are going to set goals, make them realistic. ***"Write the vision and make it plain"*** (Habakkuk 2:2; KJV).

Date _____   **Day 6**

Don't focus on the problem. Focus on the promise.
-Pastor Chad Rowe

"Being confident of this very thing, that he who began a decent work in you will perfect it until the day of Jesus Christ." (Philippians 1:6) Self-confidence is like a superhero's power for humans. When you have it nothing can take it away unless you give it away. Start by setting and achieving small realistic goals for yourself. The more you do it, the more your confidence will be boosted. The world is yours when you believe. In the Holy Bible, God set many promises, so as stated in the book of Matthew – *"Be not therefore anxious for the morrow: for the morrow will be anxious for itself"* (Matthew 6:340) – if your creator is with you, you will never be alone. Know like you know you will never be alone. That is the promise.

Date _____   **Day 7**

Our struggles may be someone else's breakthrough
. -Crystal Marie

Sometimes we may never know why or get an answer to why bad things happen to us and why we had to go through tough struggles in life. Everything happens for a reason and we are to learn the lesson and turn our tragedy into triumph even when it may hurt like hell. I've learned that my "whys" are someone else's "yeses" or answer towards the right direction. Life will throw you a curve ball, but it's up to you if you will swing at it and knock it out of the field. Experiences in life teach us how strong we are and what we can handle.

Date _____   *Day 8*

Set your soul to wisdom so that it wants nothing else.
-Lysa Terkeurst

Wisdom attracts more wisdom. Seek wisdom everyday all day and I promise it will show up. The smarter the people in your circle, the smarter you will become and, soon, only wisdom will reveal itself in you. I'm not saying foolish things won't happen, but learn from those lessons too. Seek wisdom in every situation. Even in your worst circumstances, there are lessons to be shared to help someone else coming behind you. Hence, the military has many books on "Lessons Learned". Had they not made the mistakes and/or failed at things, there would be no need for a book as such. However, a negative transformed into a positive was birthed. AHA! Today, look for the wisdom in all things.

Date _____   *Day 9*

Each morning we are born again. What we do today is what matters most.
-Buddha

Staying in the present moment is key to living the happiest life. As we have heard the saying that tomorrow is not promised, we must reflect on that statement and live for today. According to Therapist Aid, being in the now is like "paying attention in a particular way, on purpose, in the present moment, and non-judgmentally." This is called mindfulness meditation. It helps you to notice present current emotions, process them in the now, and learn to let them go. Practicing staying in the now, present or current moment is beneficial to our health also. The practice of mindfulness meditation reduces stress in our life, depression, and anxiety. Start your morning fresh each day with mindfulness meditation, learning to stay in the present moment. Your day will be better and calmer as you practice living in the present moment, recognizing emotions and processing them in a healthy way.

Date _____   ***Day 10***

For wisdom is more precious than rubies, and nothing you desire can
compare with her.
-Proverbs 8:11 KJV

Rubies are formed from a rock which are only found in rare places on just about three continents. The ruby is taken from the rock and heated in order to take out impurities and to make it shiny and strong. A ruby is a beautiful red gem. Most people born in July really adore her. If wisdom is more precious than that; What is the text saying? I'll sum it up for you. Not everyone will pay for wisdom, however, those who will have more value in their possession than anyone with a thousand rubies.

Date _____   ***Day 11***

Be intent upon the perfection of the present day.
-William Law

Being intentional produces results. Whether positive or negative, what we put our focus on is what we will most likely get. So place your focus on the positive things in your life and try your best to get the desired outcome of true happiness. When you set goals, be intentional about the steps you are going to take to achieve those goals. To be intentional you have to declare and write down your goals, dreams, or desires. Do your best in everything you do. Give your complete self into your dreams, because you are your biggest supporter to developing the "complete" best you!

Date _____   **Day 12**

> *What we like to think of ourselves and what we really are rarely*
> *have much in common.*
> -Stephen King

When you want to know the truth about yourself, don't ask yourself. You'll find that what you think of yourself and what others think of you are totally different. A wise person once said, if you want to know what you're good at ask your loyal friends. Others see the good in us that we don't always see in ourselves. It's hard for us to even talk about ourselves. Think about it. When we are asked to say something about ourselves we stutter, stall and get nervous, but when we are asked to speak of anyone else we write an entire book about the person. Allow what you think about yourself and what you really believe about yourself to have much in common.

200

Date _____   **Day 13**

Begin at once to live, and count each separate day as a separate life.
-Seneca

Each day, we can start new and fresh. Live each day to the fullest like it's your last time because tomorrow is not promised. Start living now and living your dreams. Think of every day as a new beginning to do things better than the day before, and a new day to create and experience your ambitions and goals in life. I've learned that each breathe and moment we live is precious and can be gone in a blink of an eye, with no warning. Say Hallelujah to each day! Have a grateful heart for being able to begin again. No matter what happens, keep going even if you have to begin over and over!

Date _____   **Day 14**

Use your faith to take action.
-Angela Rye

Don't depend on a chair more than you depend on yourself. When you sit down in a chair, you reflexively trust that the manufacturer has put all the parts in place correctly to hold you once you place your derriere in it. Live life knowing that the Universe has your best interest in mind. As Nike says, "Just do it" and depend on your faith to help you overcome it. When you practice faith, things happen through you and for you and not to you. When you practice faith, circumstances set you up and not set you back. When you practice faith, you stand firm in your belief of God's plan for your life and not steadfast in your comfort of the world.

Date _____   **Day 15**

Always hold fast to the present. Every situation, indeed every moment, is of infinite value, for it is the representative of a whole eternity.
-Johann Wolfgang von Goethe

Stay in the present moment. Being in the present moment means being aware of your surroundings, thoughts, and noticing them non-judgmentally. Staying in the present helps us to focus on our future and not live in the past. We can't change the past, hence, we need to focus on the things we can control, like our emotions, behavior, and our thoughts. We are who we are because of what we meditate and focus on. Focus on the positive moments in the now. Every minute of every day counts and should not be wasted. Being in the present helps you to achieve your dreams and goals faster. It puts things into perspective. It allows us to be truthful and honest with ourselves in that current moment.

Date _____   ***Day 16***

Pray for triumph over trouble.
-Matthew Knowles

Be careful with words, truly, they have power over you and the surprising thing is you have no control over what happens next. What you say can and will happen especially if you believe the things you are saying. I encourage you to pray for what you want versus what you don't want to happen. Speak positive affirmations over negative situations. Instead of saying "I hope I don't lose" say "I will win", "I can't take it anymore", say "I am more than a conqueror". Don't pray for what's wrong, pray for what's right.

Date _____   *Day 17*

We learn wisdom from failure much more than from success.
-Samuel Smiles

Learn the lesson from your failures and mistakes and find positive experiences to meditate on. Several of my shortcomings have been viewed as tragic or devastating. However, in the mist of all the pain and hurt and disappointment, I had to learn to forgive the offender, let go and find something positive to draw from the situation. Finding positive lessons from horrible situations or events in our life is often difficult for many people to do. I found that practicing mindfulness meditation on a daily basis has been beneficial to the letting go process. Life can be really hard and rough if we continue to stay stuck in negative emotions and vibes. Learn the lesson and receive the blessing!

Date _____   *Day 18*

We ought not to look back unless it is to derive useful lessons from past errors and for the purpose of profiting by dearly bought experience.
-George Washington

The past should only be examined if you are helping someone come out of a situation you once were in. The present is most important right now. The only benefit of the past is learning from it, but never be afraid of it. If failure was the past it doesn't have to be the future. If rejection was the past it doesn't have to be the future. Change the way you think and you'll change your life forever. A wise person goes back into the past only to revisit clues to better their future.

Date _____   **Day 19**

The glory is not in never failing, but in rising every time you fail.
-Chinese Proverb

Successful people understand that in order to get one "yes" you may have to hear ten "noes". Don't focus on failing but on all the positive things you can achieve. Thinking positive helps you to keep your eye on the prize of accomplishing all your dreams. Being ambitious and optimistic is key to success. Focus on the hustle and grinding of making it to the top. Don't look back; don't dwell on past mistakes because it will get you stuck and waste your time. As long as you are making progress towards success, it doesn't matter if you have setbacks. I've learned that in this life there are no free passes to the road of easy. Everything you have is because of what you have been saying and doing. So get to grinding!

Date _____   ***Day 20***

You are much more likely to regret what you don't do in your life than what you do, so give everything a try.
-Wayne Dyer

Most people are afraid to step out on their dreams, afraid of success, afraid of failure. But my only fear is what happens if I don't try. We know that if you do nothing then nothing happens. If you try, you stand a good chance of success happening. Being afraid of success is just as serious as being afraid of failure. It's all about being purposeful. When you find your true purpose for existing, it's not so hard to get out of bed because your purpose and your goals will motivate you to get up and do something. Today, seek to find the things that motivate you and wake you up to live.

Date _____   *Day 21*

Don't overlook baby steps because the big ones look more attractive.
-MaCayla Rowe

Often we are fooled by the steps it took the successful to get where they are. We allow the media and social media to shape our mind especially in thinking the rich and successful just woke up rich one day. "Stay woke" people. Trust your process, baby steps mean setting realistic goals for yourself that you can achieve. Think about when a baby learns to walk, they push themselves up by any means necessary, stand on their wobbly two feet, take one step, fall, until eventually, they walk across the room, their legs get stronger, and before you know it, they are running to those places they want to go. You can do the same right now, crawl, stand, step, run, leap all the way up the ladder of success.

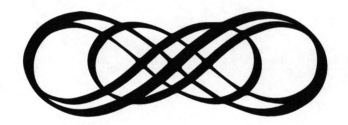

RELATIONSHIPS

Date _____   *Day 1*

A true relationship is two imperfect people refusing to give up on each other.
-Author unknown

When two people decide to come together for a relationship, they both are bringing two different perspectives, with flaws and the expectation of taking a risk to see if this thing called a relationship will work. Being in a relationship is about intentional work and effort to build a loving positive bond. No one said that it would be easy to love another person through, imperfections and differences, however, love with openness, understanding, and with the continual ability to grow together. Once you understand that both parties in the relationship are imperfect then look at yourself and ask the question, "how may I have caused conflict in the relationship and how can I improve?" We can't fix anyone in a relationship but ourselves. Identifying our emotional patterns can help with the "why" questions. Psychologist Tara Bennett-Goleman stated that "the habits we bring to a relationship come from our past experiences and disappointments. We're trying to get those needs met in our current relationship, so we place a lot of expectations on our partner."

You don't need someone to complete you. You only need someone to accept you completely.
-Rapunzel, Tangled

Choose friends who believe in you and your dreams. Choose friends who when the time gets rough, they won't get going. Choose friends who walk alongside you and not just say they have your back only to stab you in it. Choose friends who have the same goals as you. Choose friends that are going places you'd someday like to go. Choose friends who will remain with you lifelong, and learn from the ones who are only there for a season.

Date _____   *Day 3*

Positive and affirming relationships bring great pleasure, but poor relationships can bring deep pain.
-Gary Chapman

Healthy relationships are built upon assertive open and honest communication. A healthy relationship consists of basic qualities and characteristics. Those characteristics are respect, honesty, trust, support, cooperation, accountability, and safety. Toxic relationships are built around power and control. Characteristics of a toxic relationship are emotional abuse, intimidation, using privilege, isolation, psychological abuse, and sexual abuse. Finding a partner that is encouraging and supportive of your choices is important. Communication that is incorporated with loving statements is the driving force to healthy communication. Once your communication is healthy in a relationship you will be on your way to a thriving relationship.

Date _____   *Day 4*

A good relationship is when someone accepts your past, supports
your present and encourages your future.
-Zig Ziglar

Good friends understand how important the future is. Good Friends see the best in your present regardless of what you may have done in your past. Good friends encourage you and remind you that you have a future, a future of hope and that God has a plan for your life to prosper you (Jeremiah 29:11). Good friends like and love you, don't talk about you behind your back, and don't let anyone harm you. Good friends are gifts from God. So when you find one hold on to them and you return the favor.

Date _____   ***Day 5***

When two people are free to disagree, they are free to love. When they are not free, they live in fear, and love dies.
-Dr. John Townsend

Walking on "egg shells" in a relationship is not fun. A characteristic of a healthy relationship is showing mutual cooperation for one another by being willing to compromise in conflicts or disagreements. To attain healthy communication, both parties should listen with the expectation to gain a better understanding of the other partner. When there is a disagreement in a relationship, it is best to use reflective listening. Often times when we argue with our partner we are focused on getting our point across rather than listening. Reflective listening means restating what your partner has said in your own words before responding. When you agree with your partner you acknowledge their thoughts and ideas. It's called gaining an understanding before being understood. Continue to use reflective listening until your partner agrees you understand them. Using this technique of reflective listening will help both individuals feel like they are being heard and understood even if you disagree.

Date _____   *Day 6*

Don't settle for anybody just to have someone.
-Louise Hay

For things to begin, some things must end. Healthy relationships are bonds not easily broken. Healthy relationships are easy, fun, joyful, exciting and easy to deconflict. Issues and conflicts will arise, but it doesn't mean it has to come to end, or at the same time continue. Relationships help you grow, so, if conflicted ask yourself, am I at the forefront of the other person's mind? Is it time for this relationship to end? Is this person in my life for a reason, season or lifetime? Settle for the relationship that means you well and end the ones that don't.

Date _____   **Day 7**

Learning to listen may be as difficult as learning a foreign language, but learn we must if we want to communicate love.
-Gary Chapman

Reflective listening is a powerful tool to use to have effective communication and show that you care about what your partner is saying. Using reflections can help individuals become a better listener. When you are reflecting you are repeating back what that other person is saying to gain a better understanding. Try to take turns talking for about one or two minutes each pausing so that your partner has time to respond and think about what they want to say. There has been plenty of times I was formulating my thoughts waiting for them to pause and unload what I really wanted to say without really listening to the other person. How about bluntly cutting them off in mid-sentence? Got to love the interrupters, right? Reflective listening takes practice and can be beneficial to establishing healthy communication.

Date _____   Day 8

If you find someone you love in your life, then hang on to that love.
-Princess Diana

Love is patient, kind and familiar. I must add, true love actually is. Love is defined differently for everyone. Love is safe, love protects, love believes in something higher than self. Love has no conditions, love is playful, love makes you laugh more than it makes you cry, love enjoys time together, love chooses you first, love conquers, love is action, love listens, love spends time, love is none other than love and when it is put first it hangs on.

Date _____   *Day 9*

Without trust there is no relationship.
-Crystal Marie

Trust in a relationship is essential for the survival of the relationship. Trust is one of the basic characteristics of a healthy relationship. It means giving your partner the benefit of doubt without judgement. It means accepting each other's word without trying to disprove each other. If you are constantly playing the "private investigator" role in your relationship, there is little or no trust present. Building trust is possible but will require intentional effort and work. Stating how you feel and giving explanations is a way to start building trust. As well as meaning what you say and following through with commitments. Setting boundaries in a relationship is also helpful to build trust in a relationship.

Date _____   Day 10

There's nothing more difficult on the planet than another person.
-Stan Tatkin

If trouble makes itself a third party in your relationship, dig a hole and then get in the foxhole with that person and defeat the enemy together. Walk alongside one another, cover each other's back. In relationships, both must feel safe and secure, when that is lost it's hard to gain it back. Relationships can survive fights, but it cannot survive lack of safety. Trials may come, and so will floods, but don't be afraid of the flood; floods are designed to shift things, wash away the old and receive the new and refreshing.

Date _____   *Day 11*

We are sometimes deceived and blinded by imitational things in our life because we are too impatient to wait for the real thing.
-Crystal Marie

We live in a society of convenience or *right now* generation. Instant gratification is often looked for in relationships. We need to feel the false sense of happiness at whatever cost. Sometimes individuals will put up with a toxic unhealthy relationship because they don't want to be alone, deceiving themselves. We find ourselves making excuses for our unhealthy relationship. We have turned irrational thoughts into rational unhealthy thoughts in our minds. I like to use the term "pretending." Pretending that you have a real healthy relationship because you can't accept that fact that the person you are with may not be the "one." With patience comes the real thing!

Date _____   *Day 12*

The meeting of two personalities is like the contact of two chemical substances: if there is any reaction, both are transformed.
-Carl Jung

When two people come together and agree on one thing, there is so much power between the two. The mind is energy and can move things literally when put to work. Therefore, when great minds come together and think alike, no force can reckon with it. It's precisely the reason why accountability partners and masterminds are important to have, they keep you honest and focused on your dreams and goals. *"For where two or three are gathered together in my name, there am I in the midst of them"* (Matthew 18:20; KJV).

Date _____   *Day 13*

To have a healthy relationship means you have to first love yourself.
-Crystal Marie

Self-love is important to having a successful relationship. As I have mentioned in earlier quotes that we teach people how we want to be treated. That means, if you don't know how to treat and love on yourself, how can we expect our partner to know how to treat us and love us the way we want? Self-love or self-worth can be built by positive journaling, positive thinking as well as writing positive affirmations about yourself daily. When you begin to love yourself, then you can teach your partner your likes and dislikes and set your core values and boundaries within the relationship.

Date _____   ***Day 14***

They may forget what you said, but they will never forget how you made them feel.
-Carl W. Buechner

One of the sweetest gifts a person could have is that friend who listens carefully and then speaks wisely. You can recite every kind word in the dictionary, but if there is no passion and love in your delivery, it may not give life to a situation. Be the person that can speak life into those who feel like they are scum, or to the ones who don't see themselves worthy of love. A basic responsibility of people is to make others feel the "special" they've never felt before and the best reward is seeing how one simple gesture made them feel. The smile on their face while witnessing the confidence in others that they may have lacked themselves. There is safety in kind and nurturing words.

Date _____   *Day 15*

A healthy relationship starts with effective communication. Assertive communication is an essential skill for developing and maintaining healthy relationships and self-esteem.
-Crystal Marie

Assertive communication means standing up for your wants and needs as well as respecting the needs and wants of the other individual. It's about using 'I" statements to express your feeling and needs in a respectful positive way. Assertive communication involves the willingness to compromise and find a win-win solution for both individuals. According to Therapist Aid, characteristics of assertive communication are clearly stating your needs and wants, keeping eye-contact, listening without interruptions, appropriate speaking volume, steady tone of voice, and confident body language. In addition, some tips for assertive communication are respect for yourself, expressing your thoughts and feelings calmly, planning what you are going to say, and being able to tell others "no" when you need to.

Date _____   *Day 16*

Assumptions are the termites of relationships.
-Henry Winkler

"When you assume you make an *ass* of yourself", a famous line often quoted in the Army. If you don't know much or anything about something you are taking a chance of being wrong. A wrong guess will eat away at you little by little because being wrong is guaranteed to lower your self-confidence. We like to falsely accuse ourselves of not being able to achieve the very heights of our expectation, which at one time we were vulnerable to while Dreaming Big. Absolutely, never place value in opinions of others who don't believe in themselves.

Date _____   **Day 17**

Each day is an opportunity to share our hearts, our love, and our lives to the fullest. Sometimes that means just making the most out of the smallest things—like listening to each other, holding each other's hand, or just being together.
-Star Nakamoto

As a relationship continues, sometimes, we take for granted our loved ones. When we practice gratitude in a relationship it shows our partner that we appreciate them, thereby, improving the quality of our relationship. There are several gratitude tips that can be practiced on a daily basis. Showing interest in your partner's life can prove to increase closeness and effective healthy communication. Simply asking your partner how their day went is essential to a thriving relationship. Giving compliments is another way you can show your partner gratitude. If your partner likes surprises, surprise them with something special. Giving them the evening off if they have chores or other house duties can be appreciated. How about helping your partner to relax when coming home from a long day of work? Showing appreciation to our partner should involve spending quality time enjoying something you both like.

Date _____   *Day 18*

Don't smother each other. No one can grow in the shade.
-Leo Buscaglia

Precious, delicate flowers need sunlight to grow and lots of it. Appreciate the bright light in your life. We always look for shade while running from the burn of the sun, however, in some situations, you must let it burn. Roses grow while receiving the best sunlight the day has to offer, it just can't live without it. Some buds might peak in, but it will never reach its full potential. With the sun it will grow and bloom into something so special. In life, you will soon have to do the same, come from out of the shadows, in my Shirley Latour's voice, and walk into your best life!

Date _____   *Day 19*

When we understand the connection between how we live and how long we live, it's easier to make different choices. Instead of viewing the time we spend with friends and family as luxuries, we can see that these relationships are among the most powerful determinants of our well-being and survival.
-Dean Ornish

Showing consistent gratitude for our relationships and appreciating the small things will allow our relationships to flourish and grow. Gratitude brings a sense of closeness in our relationships. When we are spending quality time with one another, let's savor the moment as if it were our last time. Appreciate the time we have together and recognize that it won't be forever. Cherish your loved ones and love on them while you can and remember every moment because tomorrow's not promised. Love unconditionally, with no judgement and life will bring you the most beautiful experiences. Fellowship with our loved ones is an important part of living a long life.

Date _____   ***Day 20***

Nobody can hurt me without my permission.
-Mahatma Gandhi

Are you kidding me right now? — the question I ask people in my head that try and infiltrate my peace. I laugh inside and continue with the mission set forth before me. People can only upset you with your permission. You say yes by going into whole irate mold on them. Let your response be "Noooooo, No, No (in Amy Winehouse's voice). You control everything that happens to you and for you. Stop believing the lies told by someone that doesn't know their tail from their head. You believe the promises of God and never forget whose you are.

Date _____   *Day 21*

Our greatest power lies in our ability to heal our relationship hurts.
As we do that, we will be able to make an even greater impact on
the world.
-Shirani M. Pathak

Sometimes it's hard to let go of hurts and forgive all the wrong doings of others. Unresolved hurts cause relationships to be stagnated and stuck. When we are good, then our family and friends can be good. Self-awareness is key to thriving in a healthy relationship. To be effective and helpful to others one must be stable on the inside and secure. Then can we be more successful in life and ultimately in the world.

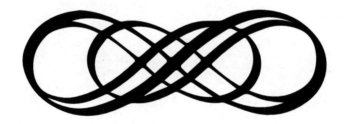

POSITIVE
WELL-BEING

Date _____   ***Day 1***

Positive thinking is the key which unlocks the doors of the world.
-Samuel Mchord Crothers

The more we think positive is the more opportunities make themselves known to us. Most people would like to be around other people that think positive because they are giving off positive vibes. When we receive positive vibes it makes us feel good and full of hope and possibilities. It's like saying the glass is half full instead of have empty. We have the power to create the world in which we live in; so thinking positive can bring a wealth of options. Developing positive thinking is a prerequisite in becoming successful in this life. Meditating on positive things such as quotes, Scriptures, listening to positive music or podcasts are a start. Just remember, positive thinking is possible, and it will open the doors of success in your life!

Date _____   *Day 2*

Today I have the power to stop doing things that are no longer working for me. -
Abeni Celeste

The definition of insanity is doing the same thing over and over and yet expect a different result. Right now, believe you have the power to change. Having a spiritual practice is putting your worries and all which troubles you into something else. You were not made to carry all your burdens. Believing in something bigger than you saves your life every day, makes you happier, and when challenges come, a spiritual practice keeps you grounded. Relying on God who is faithful gives you peace because you know and believe He has got your back. Let's practice. Repeat out loud and write as many times as you can. "I know and believe you God, Universe, Mother Nature" or whomever you believe in as long as they're a higher power than you.

Date _____   *Day 3*

Refuse to be unhappy; be cheerful instead. Refuse to let your troubles multiply; just take them one by one. Refuse to complain about things; learn to improve your surroundings. Refuse to dwell on the mistakes or disappointments that are sometimes part of life; instead learn how you can make things better. Be optimistic. Be energetic and positive about the things you do, and always hope for the best. Believe in yourself at all times and in all aspects of your life.

–Ben Daniels

You are your biggest supporter. Believing in yourself is key to being happy. Make a choice to be happy not unhappy. Find the positive in negative situations and let go of the pain of mistakes, disappointments and unmet expectations. The longer we hold on to the pain of letdowns is the longer we are stuck in the past and can't move forward. Focusing on the positive thoughts we have doesn't mean that you are in denial about the negative thoughts that will come. The beauty of it all is that you don't have to believe the negative thoughts. Challenge the negative thoughts and replace them with positive ones. Choosing to think positive and meditating on positive things eventually will spill over into who you are; so tap into that part of your brain that has the happy-thoughts and memories and use them to replace the negative thoughts!

Date _____   *Day 4*

*If you meditate you'll be a happier, more stable person, who's pro-
ductive. Because you're awake, present and thoughtful, you're good
at your job.*

-Russell Simmons

What's all this talk about being present? Meditate and I promise you'll
find out. Meditation is the answer to letting things roll downhill, for
finding it easy to "go and brush your shoulders off" (in Jay-Z's voice),
and to receive compliments that you're a Unicorn. I also find that with
meditation comes abundance. It's already within you but playing a
game of hide and seek with mediation makes it easy to find. The power of silence brings about creativity, you will find that functioning in
silence, instead of announcing everything, will leave you at peace and
a burst of energy that motivates you to dream and put some action
behind it.

Date _____   *Day 5*

Positive thinkers have twelve qualities in common: they have con-
fidence in themselves. They have a very strong sense of purpose. They
never have excuses for not doing something. They always try their
hardest for perfection. They never consider the idea of failing. They
work extremely hard toward their goals. They know who they are.
They understand their weakness as well as their strong points. They
can accept and benefit from criticism. They know when to defend
what they are doing. They are creative. They are not afraid to be a
little different in finding innovative solutions that will enable them
to achieve their dreams.
-Susan Polis Schutz

Knowing who you are is key to being positive and thinking positive.
Building positive thoughts and happiness requires intentional work.
Make a list of the things you enjoy doing that makes you happy and
that is positive and then commit to doing those things on a regular
basis. Once you build and maintain that happiness based on positive
things, you will start to think positive without realizing it. What you
think is what you will say, and what you say tells me who you are,
so meditate on positive things day and night! When we think, our
thoughts are forming our future. Negative thoughts will come, but
positive thinkers know when to shut the thoughts down because what
we think plays are part in who we become in life.

Date _____   *Day 6*

It's important to recognize that the present is the only place that living really happens.
-Deepak Chopra

Allowing your current situation to blind you and rob you of what's in front of you is you surrendering to the f-word. Nope, not that one, but Yes… even worse, yep… this one, FEAR! The art of being present is far more beautiful than any masterpiece ever drawn. The beauty in things left here by God is a gift worth waking up to every morning. I have mastered finding the beauty in everything, even in people, whether they were good to me or not. Yes, you can learn from not so good situations. Some of my worst leaders have taught me how to be a better leader. I've mastered how to make a positive environment from negative ones. God places you in what you may think is dark to bring light to the place you are in. Embrace it, and light up the room. Someone is waiting to come out of their darkness.

Date _____   **Day 7**

A defeated mind is a waste of potential.
-Crystal Marie

What we think predicts how our life may play out. If we continue to think negative thoughts, eventually our minds get stuck in a state of failure and we give up or lose motivation to become or continue in success. The battle field is in the mind. Negative thinking can be reversed with positive thoughts and meditating on positive things. Negative thoughts will come, however we don't have to entertain them; push out the negative thoughts and replace them with the positive ones. Thinking positive takes intentional effort, focus, and skill. I know it is difficult for myself as well. Practicing mindfulness to stay in the present and meditating on the positive things will conquer the defeated mind.

279

Date _____   Day 8

Whatever you say after "I am" will find you.
Joel Osteen

The game or test of life can be full of magic tricks and shortcuts. Shortcuts occur when you choose to speak life into you. For example, instead of waiting to feel beautiful before you can speak it you will say" I am Beautiful, REALLY... WOW! I am Beautiful, I am Beautiful, I am Beautiful! If repeated enough, 21 days to be exact—psychologists say habits are formed in a 21-day process and I am a witness before you—before you even know it, you will believe that you are beautiful, and folks, guess what? You're at the end of the magic show. The world knows you're beautiful already, we're just waiting on you.

Date _____   *Day 9*

Believing the impossible can be a reality.
Crystal Marie

Sometimes it is hard to believe something you can't see. Faith and hope in your dreams and passions will propel you forward. Setting goals and action steps help make dreams a reality when it could have looked hopeless. Focus on the positive things and try to find that one positive good experience even when things look hopeless. While we believe we must be patient. My faith and spiritual walk in God is what pushes me to continue on this journey in life. Knowing what you stand for and value will help make those challenging dreams a reality. Believe in yourself. That is the hard part often times. Believing that you can do the impossible was to be ingrained in your heart. This is my life's journey; continuing to believe in me no matter what people say.

Date _____   ***Day 10***

Put your slippers way under the bed at night, that way you must get on your knees to reach them in the morning.
-Denzel Washington

Good morning, Grace and Mercy! God speaks and acts at night. It is in the midnight hour that He turns a thing around. I'm so grateful He works the night shift. Due to the shift we receive at night, some situations just can't stay the same. Joy will show up, but it is only by way of thanking Him first thing in the morning. His best work is done at night. God is a night owl. I understand why my Mama and Grandma placed emphasis on saying your prayers at night. He's so faithful. It is important to get on your knees in the morning.

Date _____   *Day 11*

Choose to do the things that will reflect well… on your ability, your integrity, your spirit, your health, your tomorrows, your smiles, your dreams, and yourself.
Douglas Pagels

Do things that will represent you in a positive light. Creditability is important to success and having positive qualities will attract the right people to your inner circle. Know who you are and what you possess. Walking in honesty, truth, positive energy will take you far in life. Being positive feels good and brings a sense of hope and accomplishment. We can control who we have around us and who we surround ourselves with. Know your worth and act accordingly. Follow your passion because that will be where your purpose is and where you shine. Be the best you—the genuine you!

Date _____   *Day 12*

You are today where your thoughts have brought you, you will be tomorrow where your thoughts take you.
-James Allen

Whatever your mind makes up, your emotions will act on it. You might as well put talent to use and join all the other pursuing actors in Hollywood because your behavior will one hundred percent result in none other than those behaviors to fit your mind and emotions. I think it's the most incredible power of humans. I can make up a story, my psychic feels the emotions of my story and my actions act it all out. Aha moment for sure and the best revelation of God and the Universe. If this works for negative thoughts, wouldn't the same manifest for positive thoughts? Describe a time your negative thoughts made you feel so angry, sad or mad and you reacted in a negative way. Do the same for a positive thought.

Date _____   *Day 13*

Our own worst enemy cannot harm us as much as our unwise thoughts. No one can help us as much as our own compassionate thoughts.
-Buddha

We are what we think about ourselves. Start to think positive about your ability, who you are, and what you have to offer the world. Walk into the room as if you belong and deserve to be there. Be the majority, not the minority. Know your self-worth and excel in all the gifts God has given you. Meditate on the good thoughts, not the bad ones. There will always be those negative bad thoughts, but the good news is that we don't have to believe the negative thoughts. I have learned that successful people succeed first in their minds. If you don't believe you can do something, who else will believe?

Date _____   **Day 14**

Set yourself earnestly to see what you were made to do, and then set
yourself earnestly to do it.
-Phillips Brooks

Your purpose is far greater than any job you will hold in your entire life and, when discovered, o! What happiness and joy you'll ever be able to give yourself. Promises of living your best and fulfilled life is discovering and walking in your purpose. The answers of discovering what your purpose is are not far hidden, but you will have to seek and find them. Have you ever found someone so easily during a game of hide and seek? Did they leave tracks? Or did they make it difficult? They were found eventually, I'm sure. Either by you or by them suddenly appearing. Purpose gets revealed the same way. Let your prayer be, "Come out, come out, where ever you are".

Date _____   *Day 15*

If you have a dream, then by all means do what it takes to make it come true. If you have a goal, make it something you strive to accomplish. If you have a hope, then hope for it with all your heart.
                    -Collin McCarty

Do the work it takes to be successful. It takes intentional effort and hard work to make it in this life. Whether building a successful business, relationship, you have to do the work. Accomplishing your dreams takes patience, perseverance and resilience. The power to become a finisher requires not giving up or quitting but to keep moving, progressing even if it is with small steps. Your destiny lies in your hands and your free will to choose how you want your life story to be written. Write you goals down and set action steps to accomplish those goals. I like to say we forget thing's but paper and pen don't. Hang up your goals somewhere you can see them every day to remind you of how close you are to achieving your dreams.

Date _____   ***Day 16***

Life is a test. It is only a test. Don't sweat the small stuff. It is all
small stuff.
-Richard Carlson Ph.D.

If I'd had this epiphany at the age of 8, I wouldn't have taken life so seriously. For sure, because as a school age girl I took Test that serious. Sweat, stomachaches, anxiety and just hated the thought of test, of which, in turn, I always did so awful when it came to test. Instead of using negative emotions over things that you have no control over and even the things you do; literally laugh out loud. Situations will occur and if you believe in God, he waits to see how you will react towards that circumstance. I love the verse in the Bible that says "to whom much is given, much is required." Never react but act as if you are in control, here's a secret. People don't know the difference when you choose to play it cool but inside you're boiling, and though you know you've got this, yet you're not sweating it. Hashtag poker face. I always recite the serenity prayer in those times of distress and, magically, I feel better.

Date _____   Day 17

The greatest discovery of my generation is that human beings can alter their lives by altering their attitudes.
-William James

How we behave and act plays a part in the success we have in our lives. Good attitudes can go a long way when you want to get far in life. Think about a time when you changed your attitude to good in a bad situation, it made things a little easier to go through. How you perceive life with determine how successful you can be. I often tell others, let's start thinking and talking ourselves into positive experiences instead of talking ourselves out of things because of fear. That's it, people, we have to think ourselves happy, successful and great to make it in this life. **"As a man thinketh in his heart, so is he"** (Proverbs 23:7; KJV).

Date _____   *Day 18*

Surround yourself with good people.
-Vivica A. Fox.

Good people spread like margarine on hot toast. Good people birth other good people; a good person attracts another good person for friend. Good people are magnets and all people gravitate towards them, even the not-so-good people because they are inspired and deep down they want to be good people too. Good people aren't born they are chosen. By whom? Chosen by themselves. Choose to be well, do well and know well. The choice is always yours.

Date _____   *Day 19*

Wellness is not a 'medical fix' but a way of living – a lifestyle sensitive and responsive to all the dimensions of body, mind, and spirit; an approach to life we each design to achieve, our highest potential for well-being now and forever.

-Greg Anderson

Wellness starts in the mind. My goal in life is to be healthy emotionally, mentally, physically, and spiritually. Taking a holistic approach to wellness is my mindset for myself and others I help. To be completely healthy and whole completely requires a paradigm shift of our mind. We must live it and wellness must become one with us. Positive well-being starts with positive thinking and what we are meditating on, focusing on, and striving for, to help us get our greatest potential. Meditate on positive experiences, quotes, and surround yourself with positive people that will nurture and support you in your journey to positive well-being.

Date _____   ***Day 20***

A Dream is nothing more than a thought asking for permission to live.

-Pastor Keion Henderson

You have a choice to allow your dream to live or die. The Bible tells us there is power in the tongue. If words have life or death, isn't it rather wise to speak life-words concerning your dream? Beware of dream killers. Believe in yourself first, it's hard for others to believe in something you don't believe in. And stay away from those that can't speak life into you and those that don't mind their own business. They don't believe in you because they don't believe in themselves. Aha moment… if I can believe in me, I can believe in others. Remember, everything begins and ends with you. And you always have the power to choose. Dream bigger and then give it permission to live.

If you change the way you look at things, the things you look at change.
-Wayne Dyer

Recently, my church celebrated our Pastor's birthday. A panel of individuals spoke about a few of his most memorable sermons. One spoke of his message titled *"It's Possible."* What is possible? It is possible that a negative childhood could be what shaped you into living your best life in adulthood; it is possible that when one door closes there are others that will open and if there is no door, you have the knowledge, strength and material to build your own. Create your own opportunities when these doors close. If you can't make it to Broadway, create your own Broadway. Plant, sow, harvest throughout your life. And in the words of my Pastor, "benefits outweigh the cost" every time.

EPILOGUE

This journal was written to present our message to as many people in the world as we can. Since we know hurt people hurt people, it is our prayer to help heal people so that healed people can heal people. You can heal your mind. Life will happen, but your response will always determine the outcome. This project was nine months in the making. Just imagine the distractions, roadblocks, barriers, complications, but we didn't allow turmoil to win. We persevered, stayed focus, met up on days when the desire just was not present and I'm so glad we did because if we didn't you would not be reading this page. Affirm what you set out to do, if change is what you want in your life, speak it, believe it and start walking in it so you can see the manifestations and abundance overflowing from you onto the people around you.

NOTES

Quotes -A Daybook of Positive Thinking: Daily Affirmations of Gratitude and Happiness by Patricia Wayant.

Mindfulness Day by Day: How to Create Peace and Happiness in Your Daily Life by A Blue Mountain Arts Collection.

Acts of Faith, Daily Meditations for People of Color by Iyanla Vanzant.

The Wisdom of Sundays: Life-Changing Insights from Super Soul Conversations by Oprah Winfrey.

Bible scriptures from NKJV, KJV, & MSG versions

Information- www.therapistaid.com and www.google.com

Sermons and quotes from Pastor Chad and Marla Rowe of Destiny World Outreach Center.

ABOUT THE AUTHORS

Crystal Morris is an educator, counselor, author and mentor who inspires youth and people of all ages. She has been in the education field for over ten years working with at risk youth, young adults and mentoring women of all ages. Crystal Morris is currently a Licensed Professional Counselor and a Military Family Life

Counselor for adults. Crystal Morris is the author of *"The Butterfly Affect: Living the Single Life Through God's Eyes"*, and is currently writing the second book in the series *"The Butterfly Affect: Establishing Healthy Relationships"*. She currently spends her time with family, children and counsels professionally.

For more information from Crystal Morris please visit www.butterflies-prosperingbehavioralhealthservices.com.

Facebook:@ButterfliesProsperingBehavioralHealthServices. You can follow her also @Authorsof21DaysofPositiveLiving and Instagram 21Daysofpositive. To book Crystal Morris for speaking engagements, please use the contact form on her website or email 21daysofpositiveliving @gmail.com.

Abeni "Celeste" Scott is a retired Veteran and has a Masters of Science in Professional Counseling. Celeste and Crystal met during Celeste's internship at a local shelter for abused women. Celeste now volunteers at the same shelter and continues to work with women helping to transform their lives. She has experience in early childhood education and volunteers at a local public school as well.

Celeste is also Co-Author in a bestselling and award-winning book, *Camouflaged Sisters: Behind the Rank Vol 1*. She has spoken on several platforms and led workshops in her community to inspire and empower women to walk in their greatness. She is currently co-writing another book titled *"Thursday Talk on the Red Couch"* motivated by her Facebook community, Ilva & Celeste, the book is due Winter 2018.

You may contact Celeste at the emails below:

21daysofpositiveliving@gmail.com or abeni15@hotmail.com.

ACKNOWLEDGEMENTS

We would like to thank God for giving us strength and vision to write this journal. Thank you to our Pastor Chad Rowe for believing in us, Lila Holley for inspiration, guidance and mentorship, and Karen Vandiver for emotional support.

A special thanks to our loved ones and friends who witnessed this journey to positive living.

Thank you, daddy for being with me in spirit and motivating me to keep living positive, I love you forever ∞

Crystal

Made in the USA
Columbia, SC
20 November 2020